WORKING TOGETHER

SHARING TASKS

BY ABBY COLICH

BLUE OWL BOOKS

TIPS FOR CAREGIVERS

Social and emotional learning (SEL) helps children manage emotions, learn how to feel empathy, create and achieve goals, and make good decisions. Strong lessons and support in SEL will help children establish positive habits in communication, cooperation, and decision-making. By incorporating SEL in early reading, children will learn the importance of respect and encouragement when working with others.

BEFORE READING

Talk to the reader about the importance of sharing tasks among a group.

Discuss: Think of a time you worked on a group project. What was your job? Did you think the tasks were even and fair?

AFTER READING

Talk about how communication can make group work go more smoothly and help prevent and solve problems.

Discuss: What are some things you need to talk about when working in a group? How does communicating make you a better team member?

SEL GOAL

Children may have a difficult time understanding how to divide tasks among a group or the importance of communication in group projects. Talk to readers about accountability. When you know others are depending on you, you understand the importance of getting the job done. If a task isn't going well or if you need help, be sure to let your group know.

TABLE OF CONTENTS

CHAPTER 1

GETTING STARTED

Working in a group can be **rewarding**. You may learn how to do something new or how to work better with others. It is not always easy. But when everyone does his or her part, you can accomplish so much.

When you start a group project, make sure everyone understands what the **goals** are and when everything is due. Ask any questions you have.

CHAPTER 2

ASSIGNING TASKS

Talk to your teammates about the tasks that your group will need to do to finish the project. Figure out how long each task will take.

Try to make sure the tasks are fair. Everyone should put in an equal amount of work. Zoe's group is acting out a play. Zoe only has a few lines, so she helps with costumes.

Get to know your group members. Find out what everyone's strengths are and what tasks they are interested in. This will help the group **assign** jobs.

Ajay's group has to give a news report. Ajay is a **confident** speaker. He asks to be the host. Luis likes to write. He works on the script. Mia is **outgoing**. She finds people to interview.

TRY SOMETHING NEW

Don't be afraid to try something new, even if you don't think you're the best at it. If you are interested in a task, tell your group that you'll do your best and will ask for help if needed.

Two people may want the same job. When this happens, you'll have to **compromise**.

Stella and Rose are making a game for math class. They both want to design the game board. They decide Stella will design the board, and Rose will design the cards.

CHAPTER 3

COMMUNICATING

Good **communication** can help your project go well. Check in with your group as you work. Have everyone share what they have done so far. If you have questions, be sure to ask your teammates.

Communicating with your group can help prevent and solve problems. Let your group know of any issues that come up. Dante is having trouble finding information. He tells the group. Cody helps him.

Encourage others. This helps everyone stay **motivated**. Etta is worried she won't memorize her part in the musical by opening night. Keesha tells her she believes she can get it done. She helps her practice.

ASK FOR HELP

If you don't think you can get your job finished on time, speak up! Another team member, teacher, or adult might be able to help.

Each person in a group has a job to do. That means you all depend on one another to get the project done. Be **mindful** of your time. Give your full attention to your tasks. Don't rush.

Break up larger tasks into smaller steps. This can help a large task feel easier to complete. Naomi and her group are making a model city. They start by collecting boxes that will be the buildings.

If there are problems, show **empathy**. Malik is taking a long time to finish his task. At first, Ian is **impatient**. But he takes a deep breath. He thinks about what to say. He asks if Malik needs help. Malik says he is having trouble programming the website. Ian tells Malik he sometimes gets stuck, too. Together, they come up with an idea.

HELP OTHERS SPEAK UP

Some people may be shy or afraid to speak up. If someone in your group seems quiet, check in to make sure everything is going well.

Communicating with your team can help prevent and solve problems. When everyone works together and finishes their tasks, you can accomplish so much!

VOLUNTEER
VOLUNTEER
UNTEER

GOALS AND TOOLS

GROW WITH GOALS

Communicating with all members of your group can help your project go smoothly. What can you do to help your group work go well?

Goal: Encourage your team members. Tell them they are doing a good job. Point out what you like about the work they are doing.

Goal: If someone is struggling, ask what he or she thinks is wrong. Offer ideas on how to work through the problem. You can help with the task without doing it for that person.

Goal: Break a large task up into smaller steps. Work on one step at a time.

WRITING REFLECTION

Communication is important any time you work with others. Reflecting on past experiences can help you build communication skills.

1. Write about a time when working with others went well. How did you communicate with one another?
2. Write about a time when working with others did not go well. What were some ways that you could have communicated better?
3. What is one thing you learned about communication the last time you worked in a group?

GLOSSARY

assign
To give someone a job to do.

communication
The sharing of information, ideas, or feelings with another person through language, eye contact, or gestures.

compromise
To agree to accept something that is not entirely what you wanted in order to satisfy some of the requests of other people.

confident
Self-assured and having a strong belief in your own abilities.

empathy
The ability to understand and be sensitive to the thoughts and feelings of others.

encourage
To give someone confidence, usually by using praise and support.

goals
Things you aim to do.

impatient
Easily annoyed.

mindful
A mentality achieved by focusing on the present moment and calmly recognizing and accepting your feelings, thoughts, and sensations.

motivated
Having a strong desire to do well at something.

outgoing
Warm, friendly, and confident.

rewarding
Offering or bringing satisfaction.

TO LEARN MORE

FACT SURFER

Finding more information is as easy as 1, 2, 3.

1. Go to www.factsurfer.com
2. Enter "**sharingtasks**" into the search box.
3. Choose your book to see a list of websites.

INDEX

Blue Owl Books are published by Jump!, 5357 Penn Avenue South, Minneapolis, MN 55419, www.jumplibrary.com

Library of Congress Cataloging-in-Publication Data

Names: Colich, Abby, author.
Title: Sharing tasks / by Abby Colich.
Description: Minneapolis: Jump!, Inc., [2022] | Series: Working together | Includes index. | Audience: Ages 7–10
Identifiers: LCCN 2020057962 (print)
LCCN 2020057963 (ebook)
ISBN 9781636901268 (hardcover)
ISBN 9781636901275 (paperback)
ISBN 9781636901282 (ebook)
Subjects: LCSH: Small groups–Juvenile literature. | Task analysis–Juvenile literature.
Communication in small groups–Juvenile literature. | Social skills in children–Juvenile literature.
Classification: LCC HM736 .C647 2022 (print)
LCC HM736 (ebook) | DDC 302.34–dc23
LC record available at https://lccn.loc.gov/2020057962
LC ebook record available at https://lccn.loc.gov/2020057963

Editor: Eliza Leahy
Designer: Molly Ballanger

Photo Credits: fstop123/iStock, cover; Zurijeta/Shutterstock, 1; LightField Studios/Shutterstock, 3; FatCamera/iStock, 4; Johannes Kroemer/Getty, 5; voyata/Shutterstock, 6; Zheka-Boss/iStock, 7; Pixel-Shot/Shutterstock, 8–9; SeventyFour/iStock, 10–11; Shutterstock, 12; CREATISTA/iStock, 13; NickyLloyd/iStock, 14–15; Weekend Images Inc/Getty, 16–17; Littlekidmoment/Shutterstock, 18–19; Jose Luis Pelaez Inc/Getty, 20–21.

Printed in the United States of America at Corporate Graphics in North Mankato, Minnesota.